"Simplicity is not an objective in art, but one achieves simplicity despite one's self by entering into the real sense of things."

Constantin Brancusi

Day after day, new memories are made while older ones fade into ...

For the past decade, my work has been about observing life as a work in progress observing what remains of all our experiences as we carry on living. I want to appreciate the consequential moments that too rarely stand out against the dull routine of daily existence. More specifically I am interested in the instants that cultivate and nourish the patina of one's aging soul. To translate these ideas into paintings I experiment with the application of pigments as I do with their removal, creating marred and injured surfaces, rich as life itself, revealing traces and scars, like faded memories too stubborn to be forgotten.

I hope to evoke similar impressions to those that are best described in the Japanese aesthetic philosophy of Wabi-Sabi; the deep appreciation for the simple melancholy and beauty that is inherent to imperfection, the ephemeral and the modest, antidotes to the ever more pervasive vulgar in our world.

Thank you.

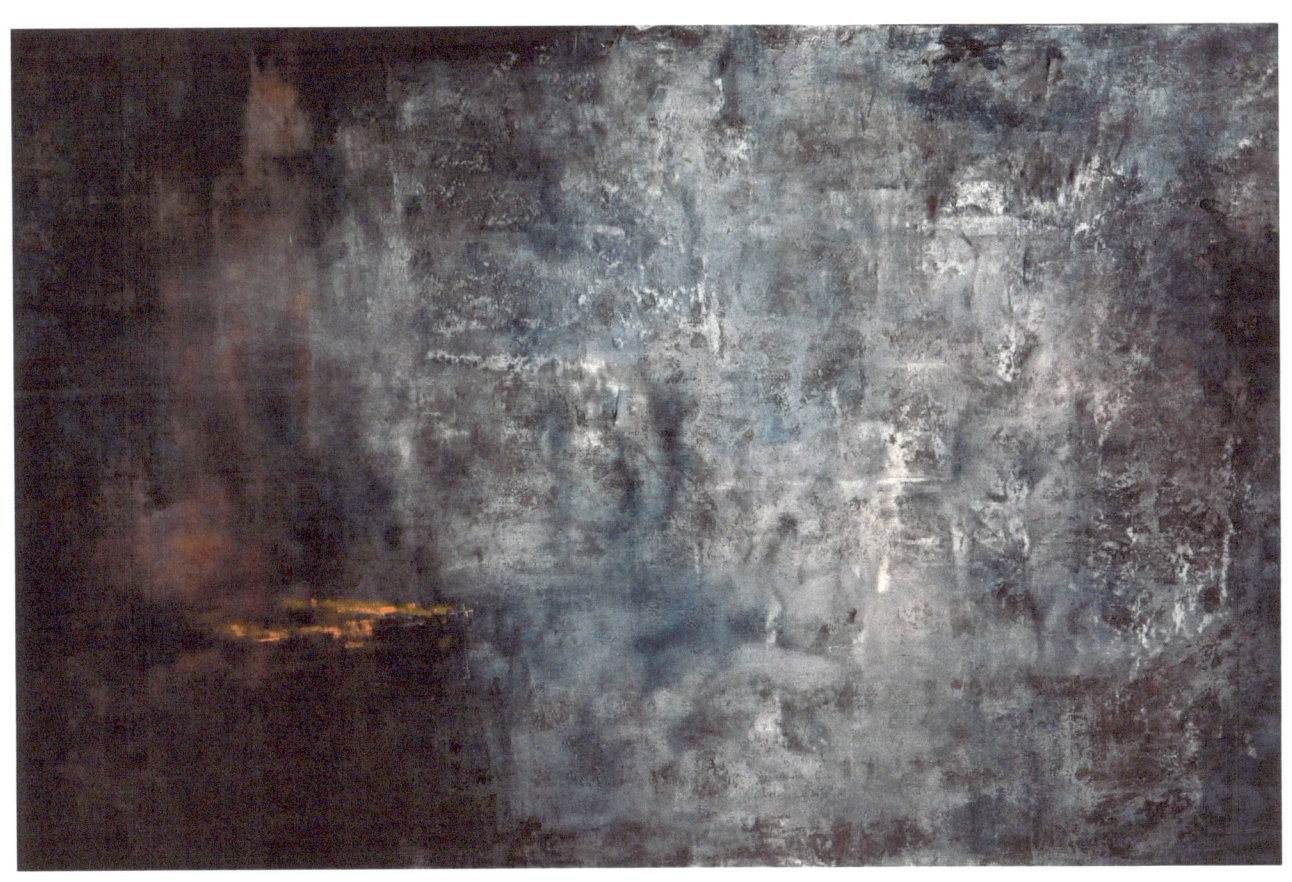

Oil on wood
200 x 120 cm
In private collection

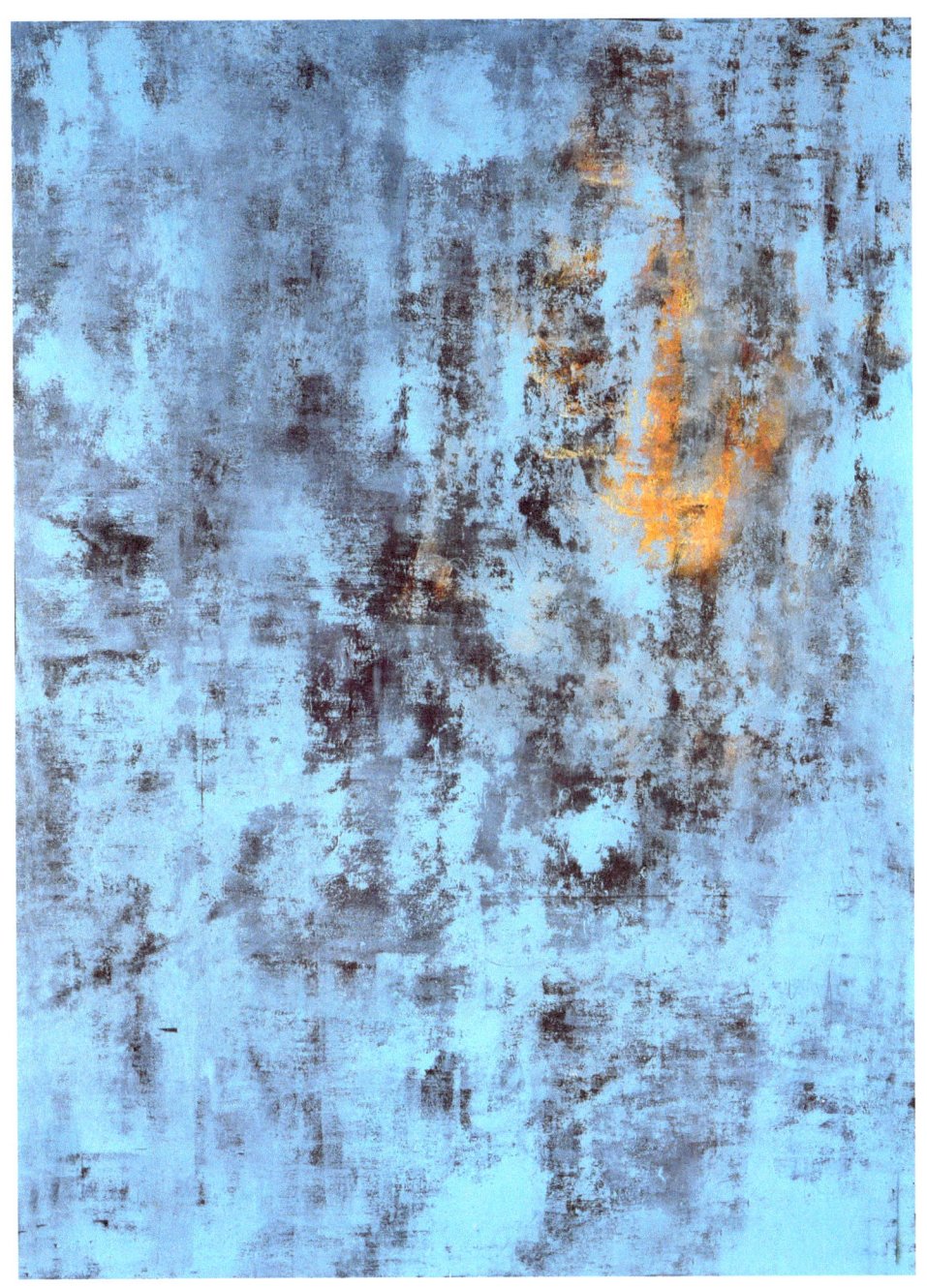

Oil on wood
120 x 80 cm
In private collection

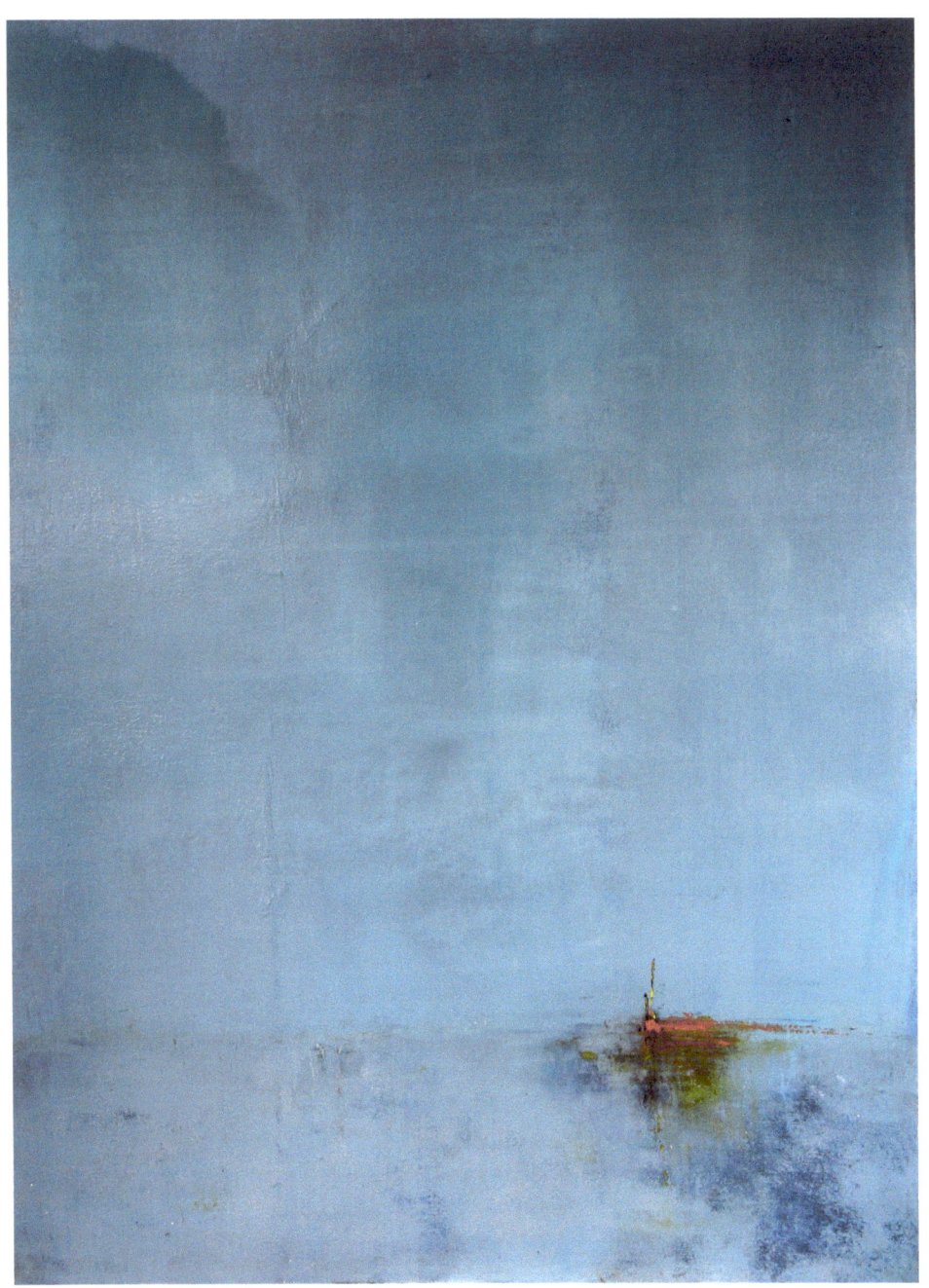

Oil on paper
77 x 55 cm
In private collection

Oil on paper
77 x 55 cm
In private collection

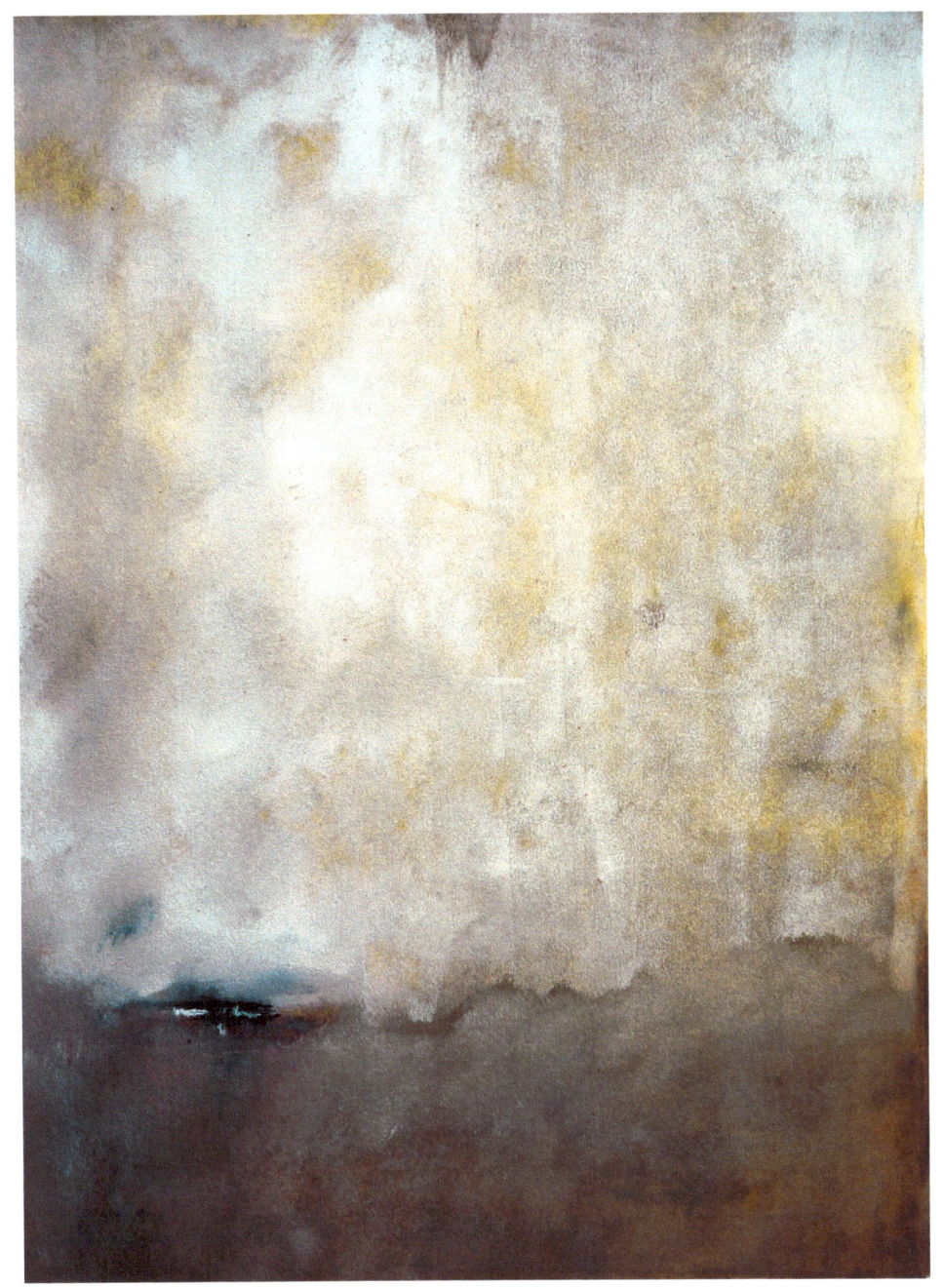

Oil on paper
77 x 55 cm
In private collection

Oil on paper
77 x 55 cm
In private collection

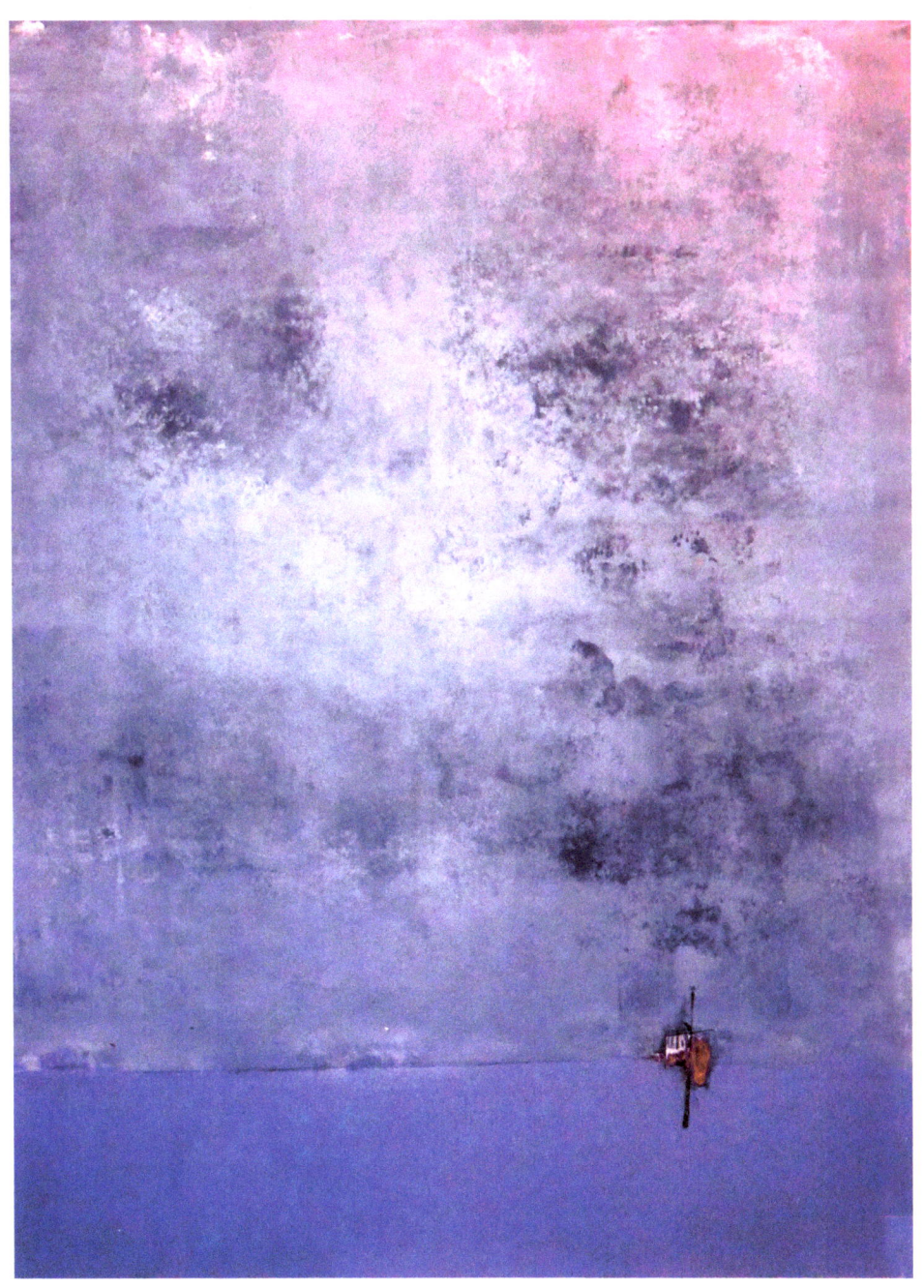

Oil on paper
77 x 55 cm
In private collection

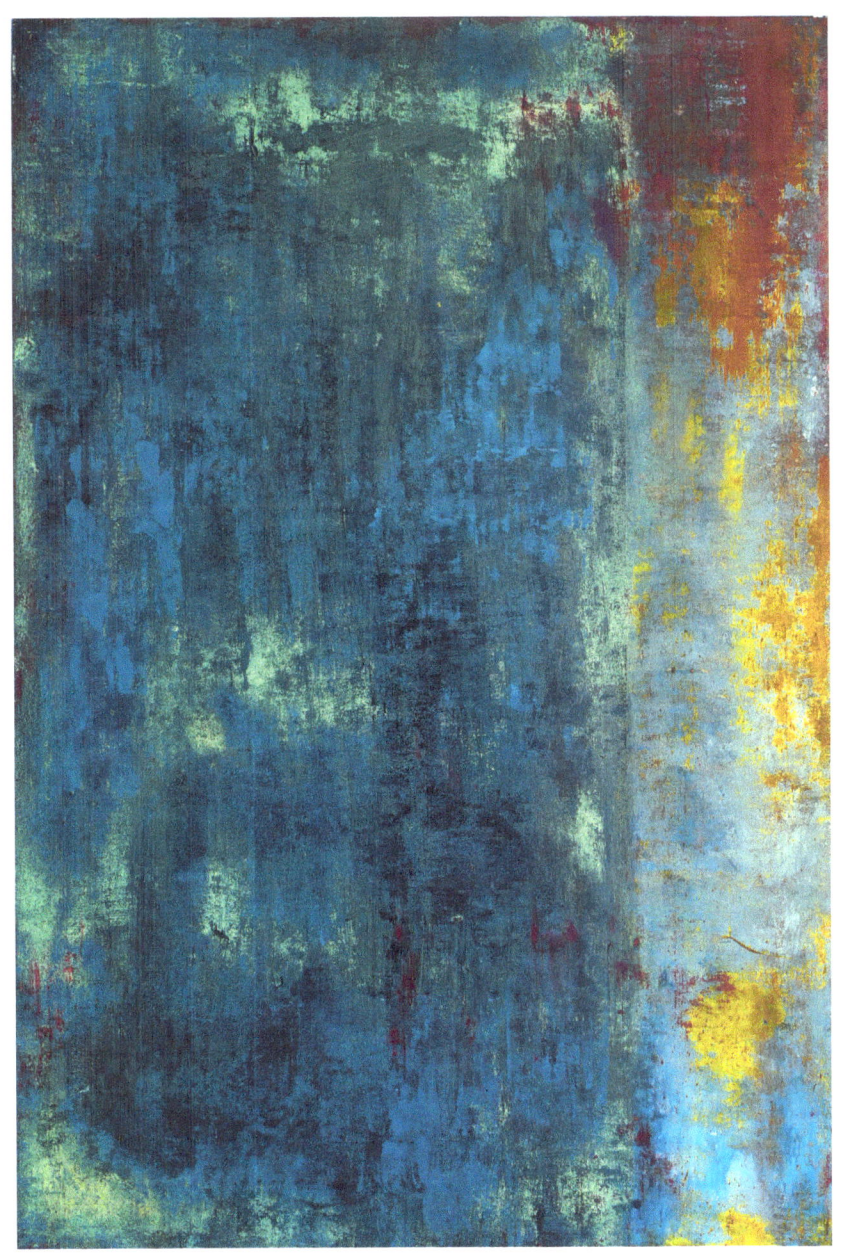

Oil on wood
120 x 80 cm
In private collection

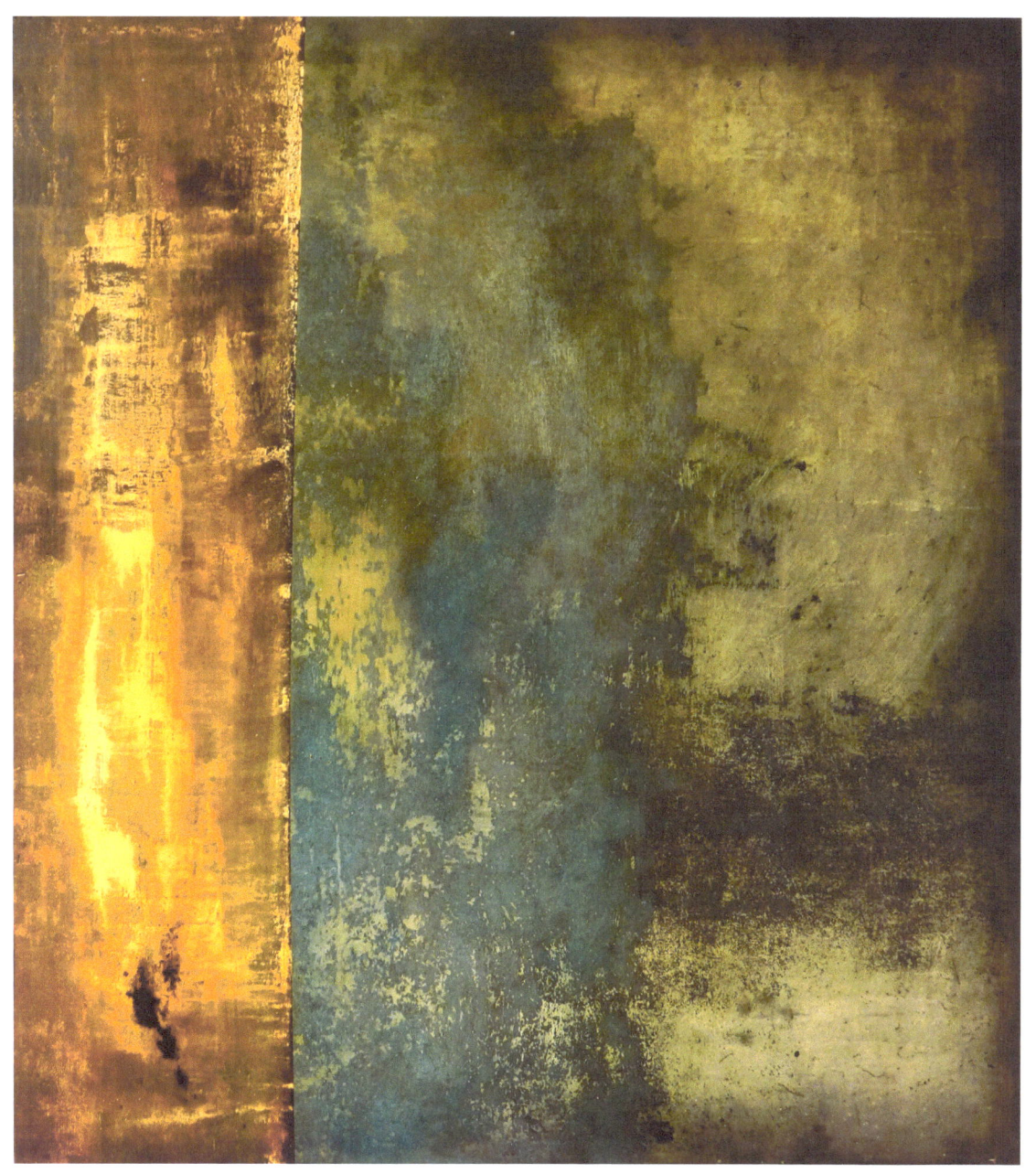

Oil and goldleaf on wood
120 x120 cm
In private collection

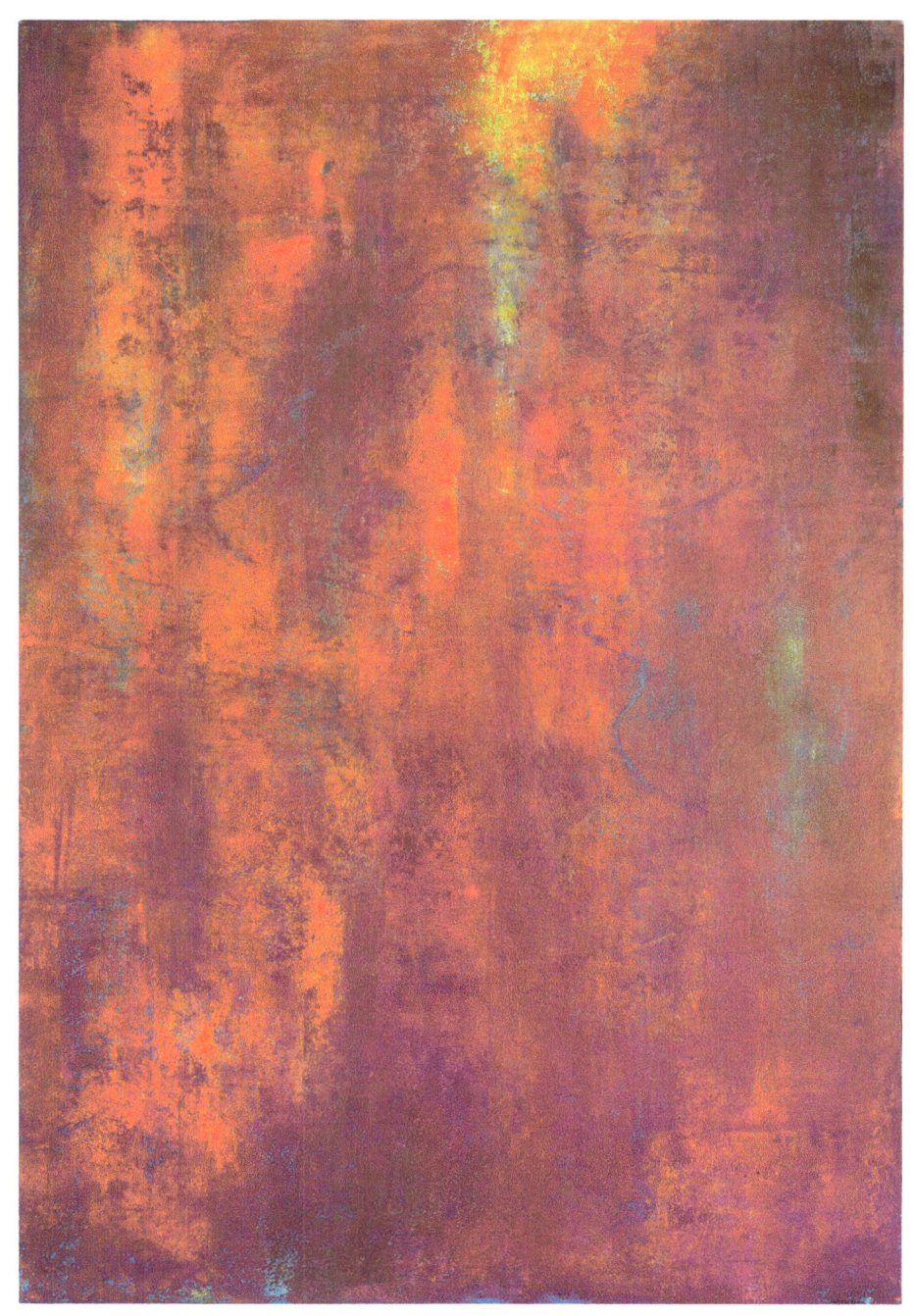

Oil on wood
120 x 80 cm
In private collection

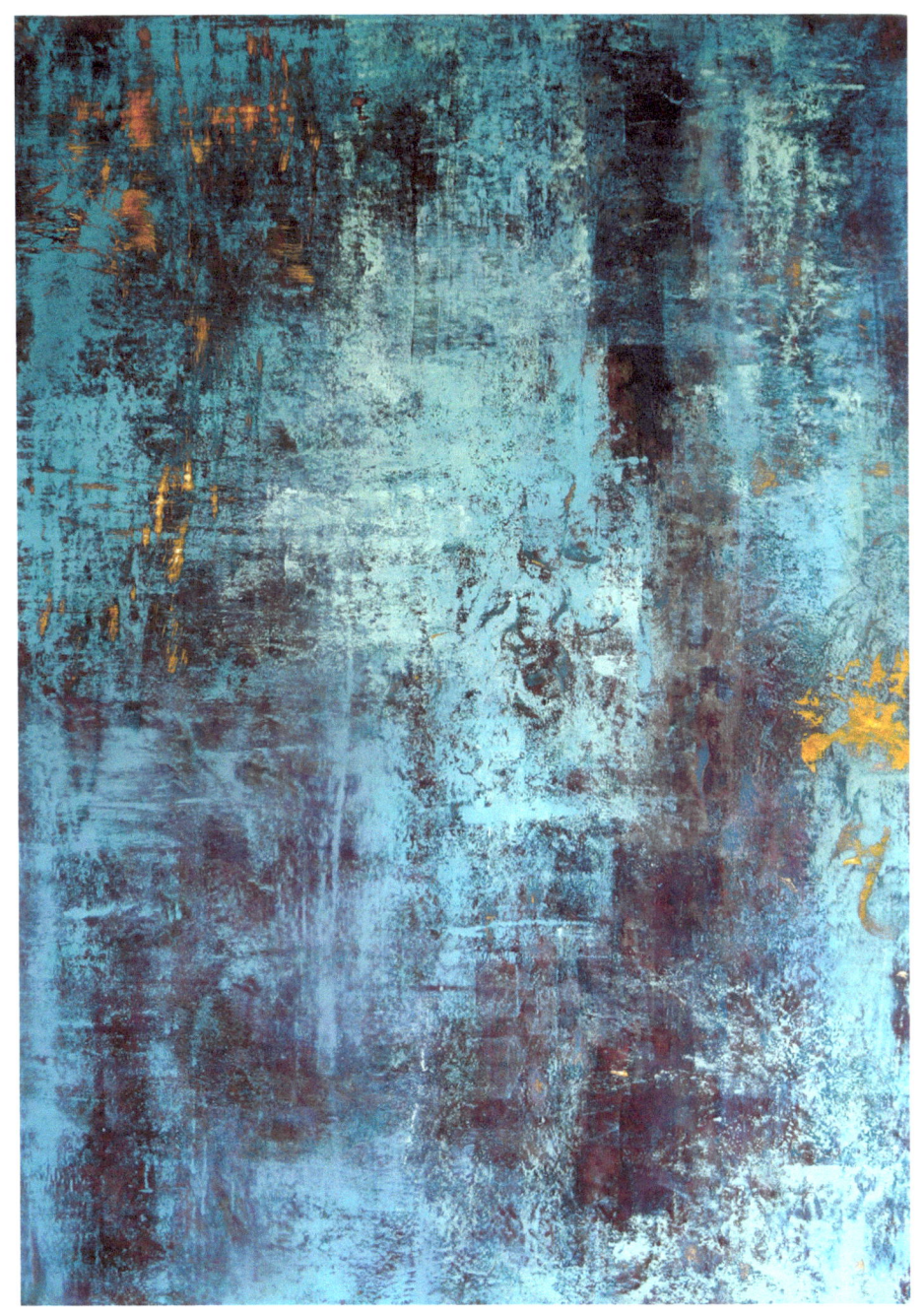

Oil on wood
120 x 80 cm
In private collection

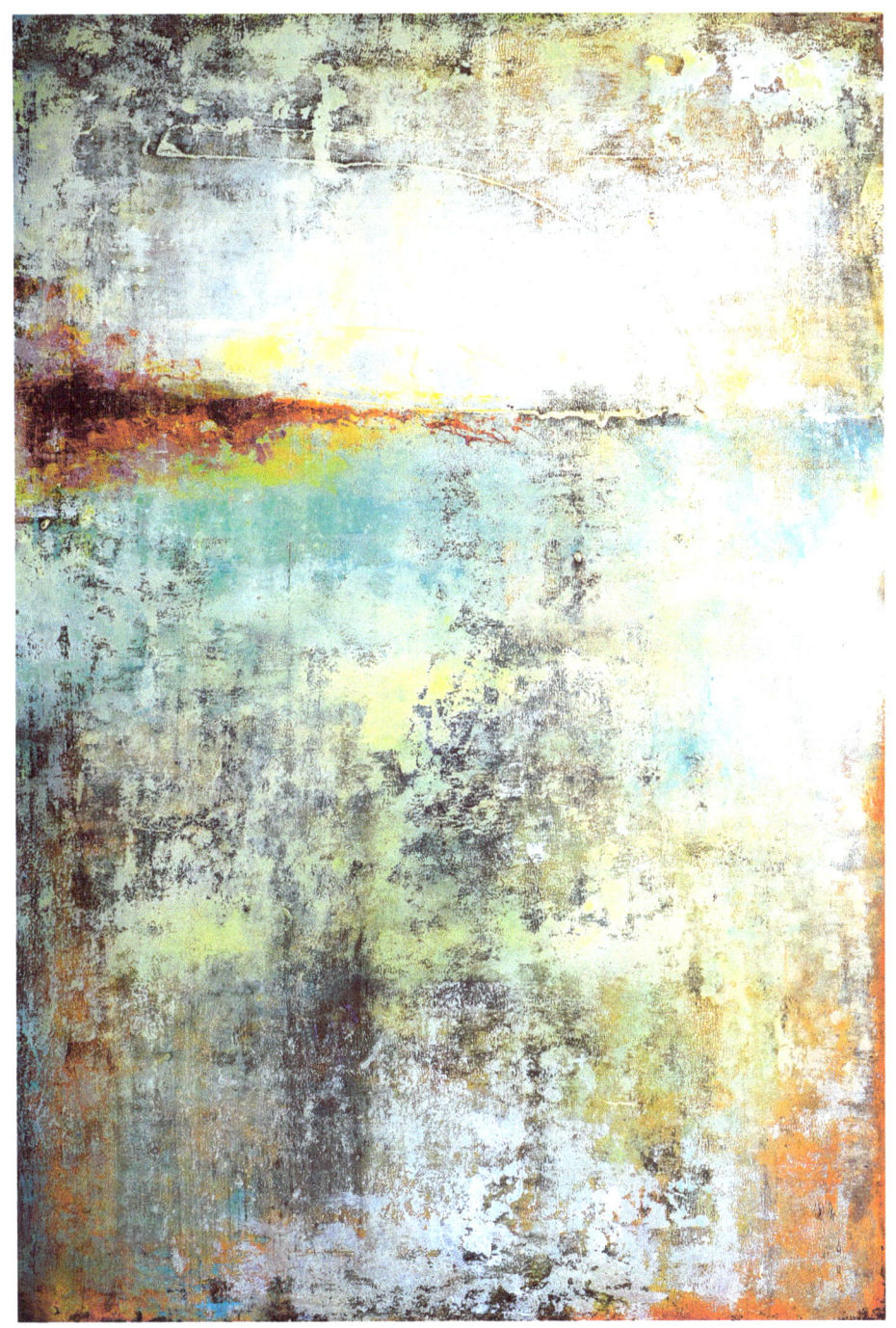

Oil on wood
120 x 80 cm
In private collection

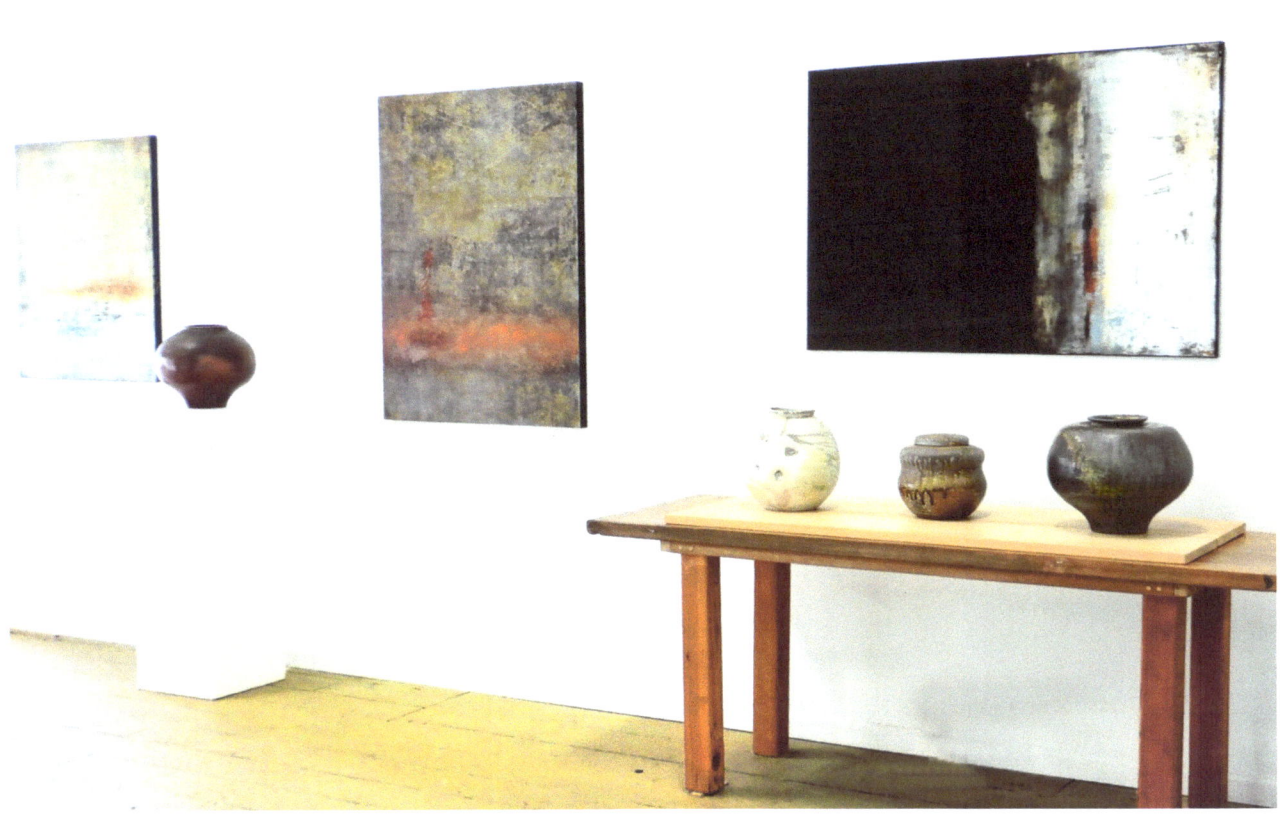

BlackFaun Gallery
"Interstices of quietude" Exhibit
2019

Ceramics by Thomas Fossier

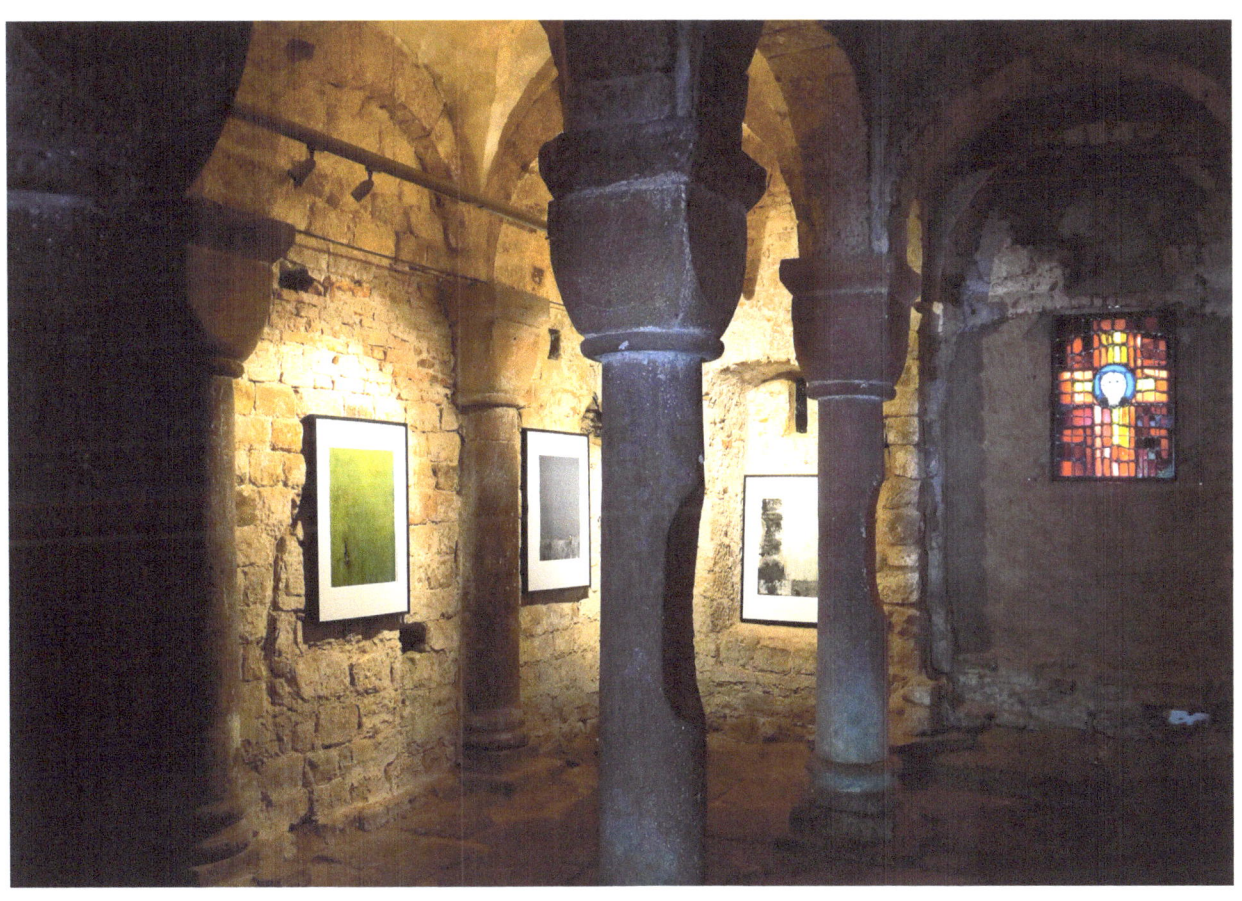

Abbatiale St Pierre et Paul, Wissembourg, France
"Un moment de doute" Exhibit
2015

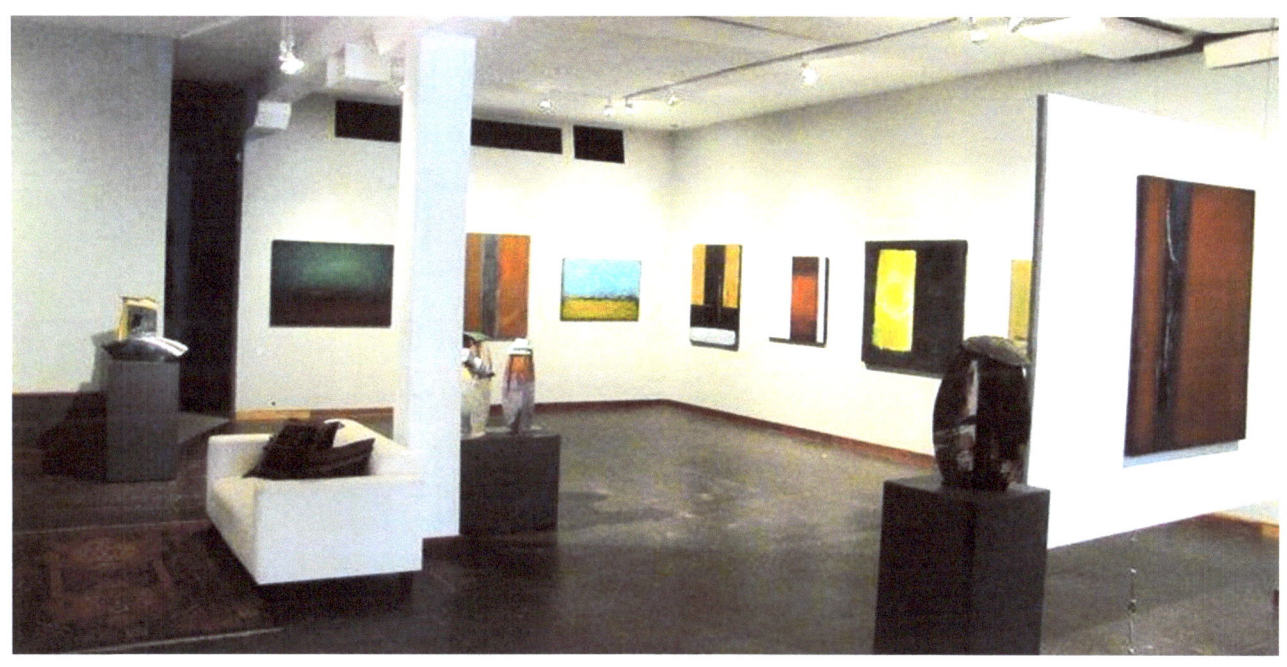

Accident Gallery
"Bedtime stories to myself" Exhibit
2008

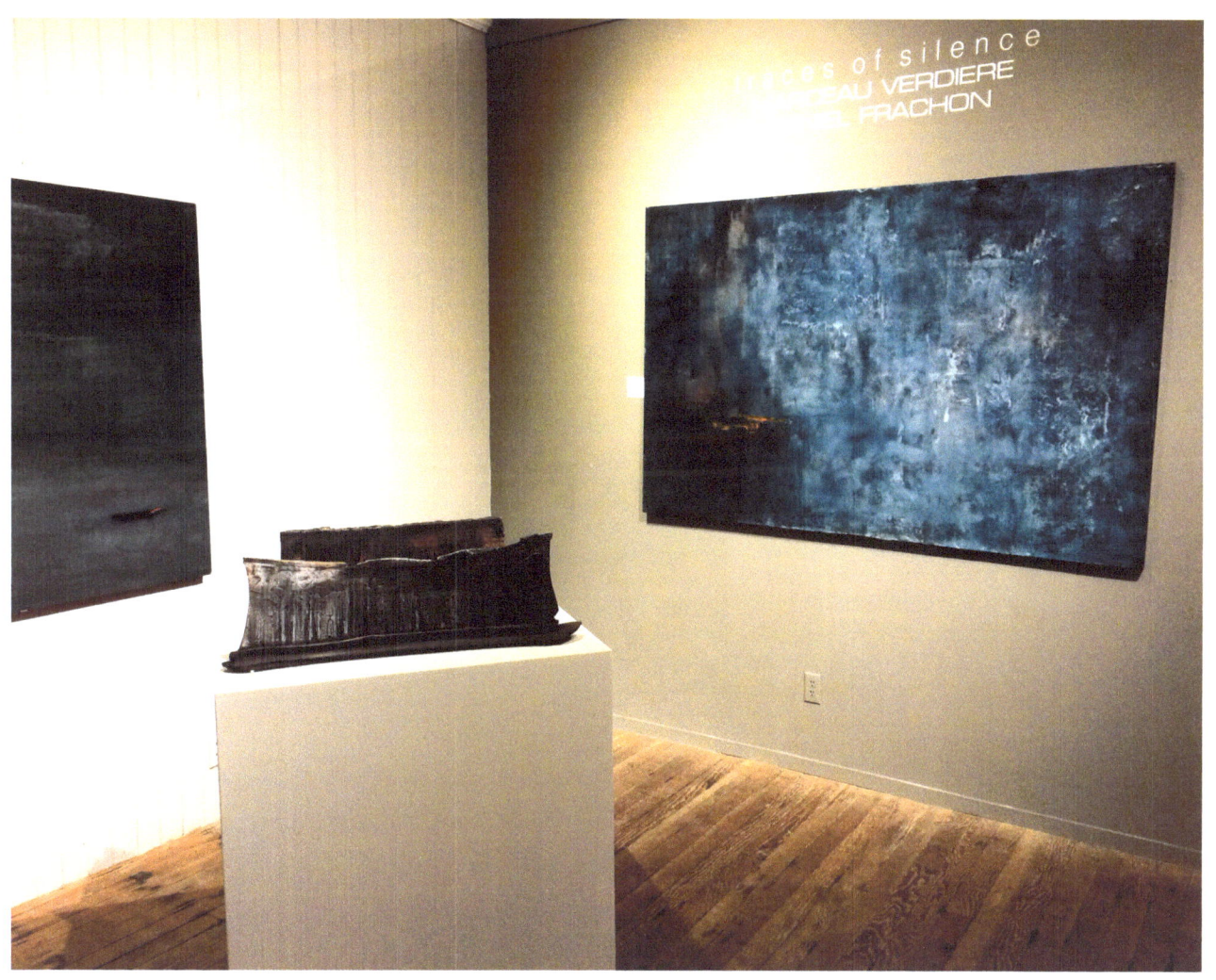

Piante Gallery
"Traces of silence" Exhibit
2016

Ceramics by Daniel Frachon

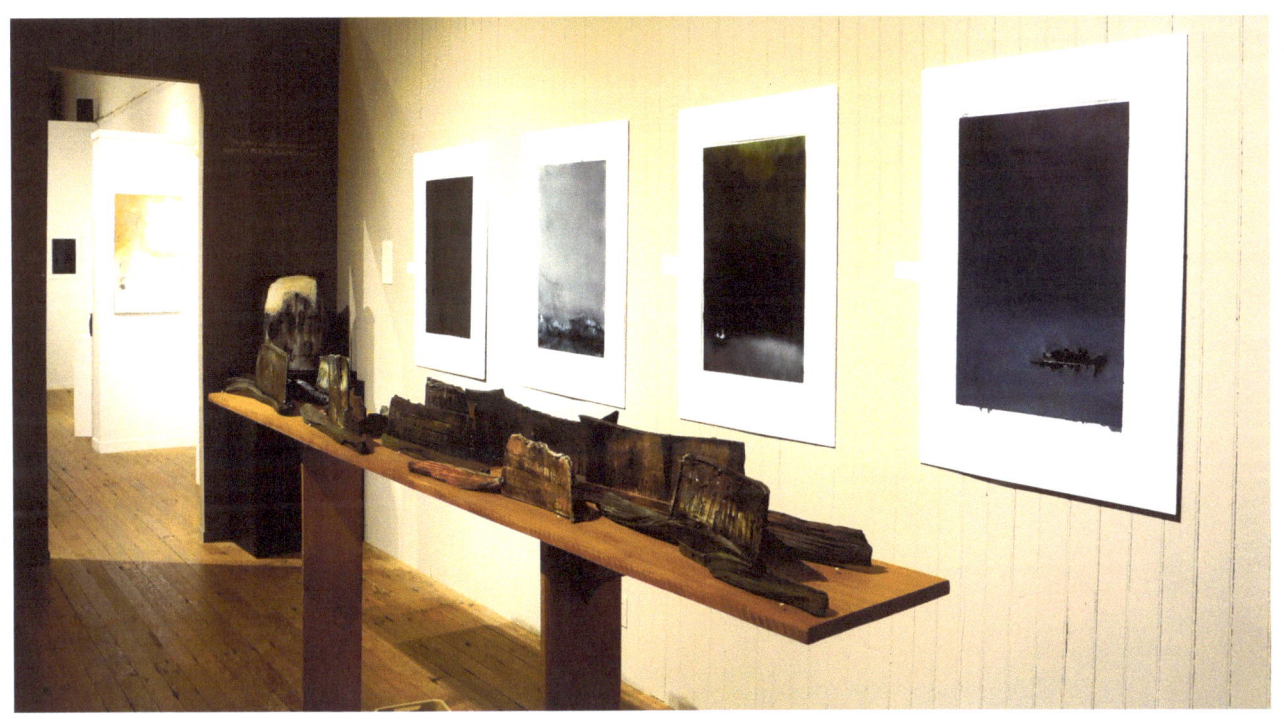

Piante Gallery
"Traces of silence" Exhibit
2016

Ceramics by Daniel Franchon

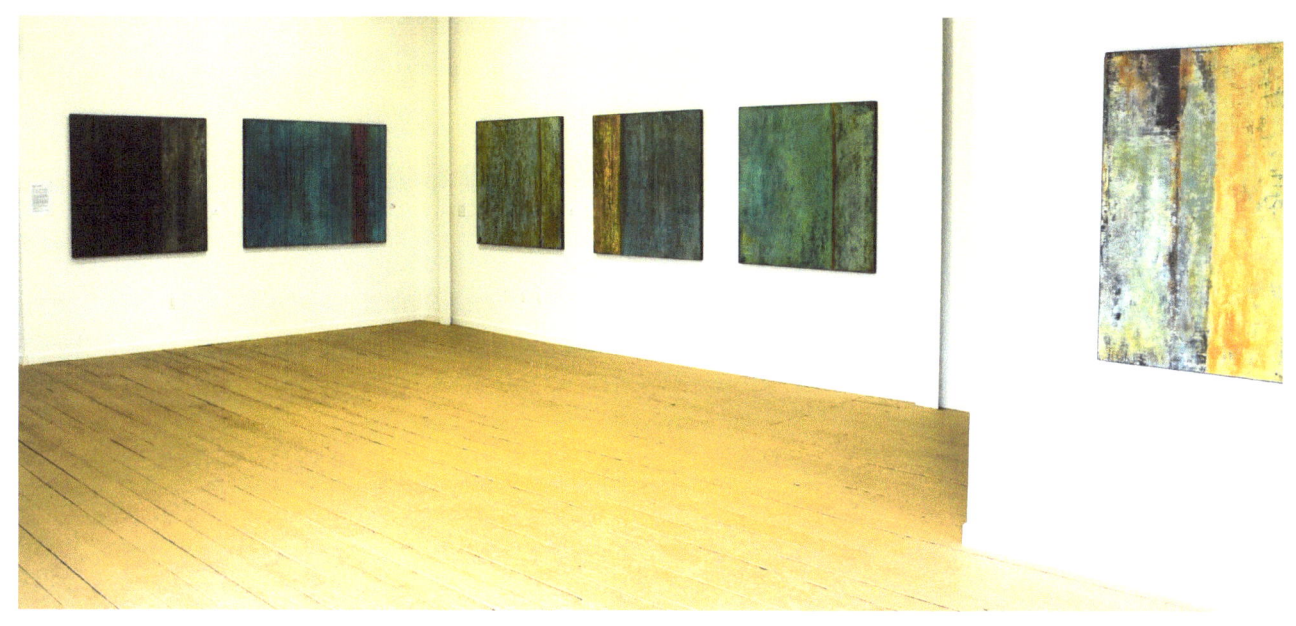

Blackfaun Gallery
"Conversa" Exhibit
2018

Oil on paper
195 x 100 cm
In private collection

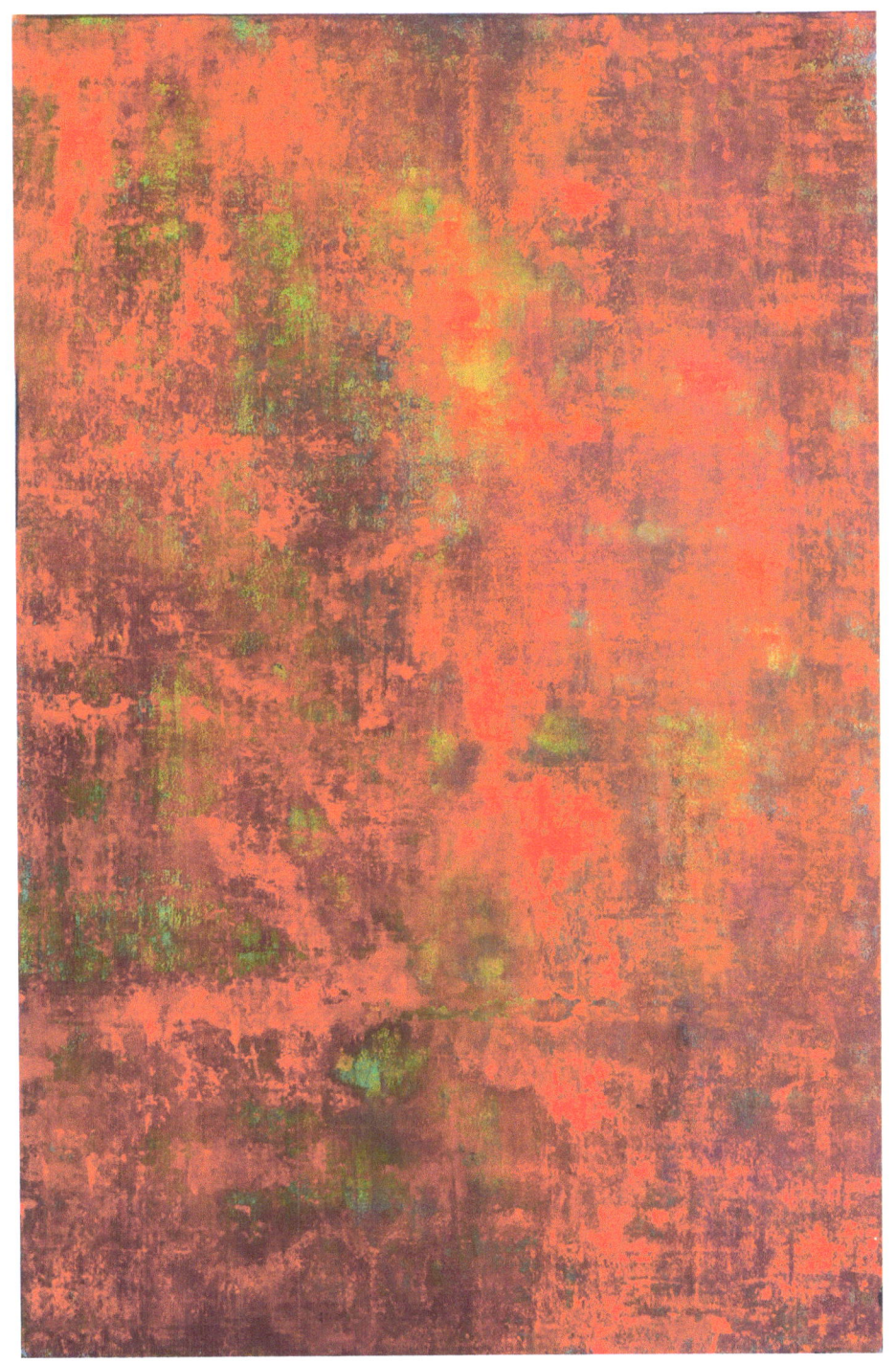

Oil on wood
120 x 80 cm
In private collection

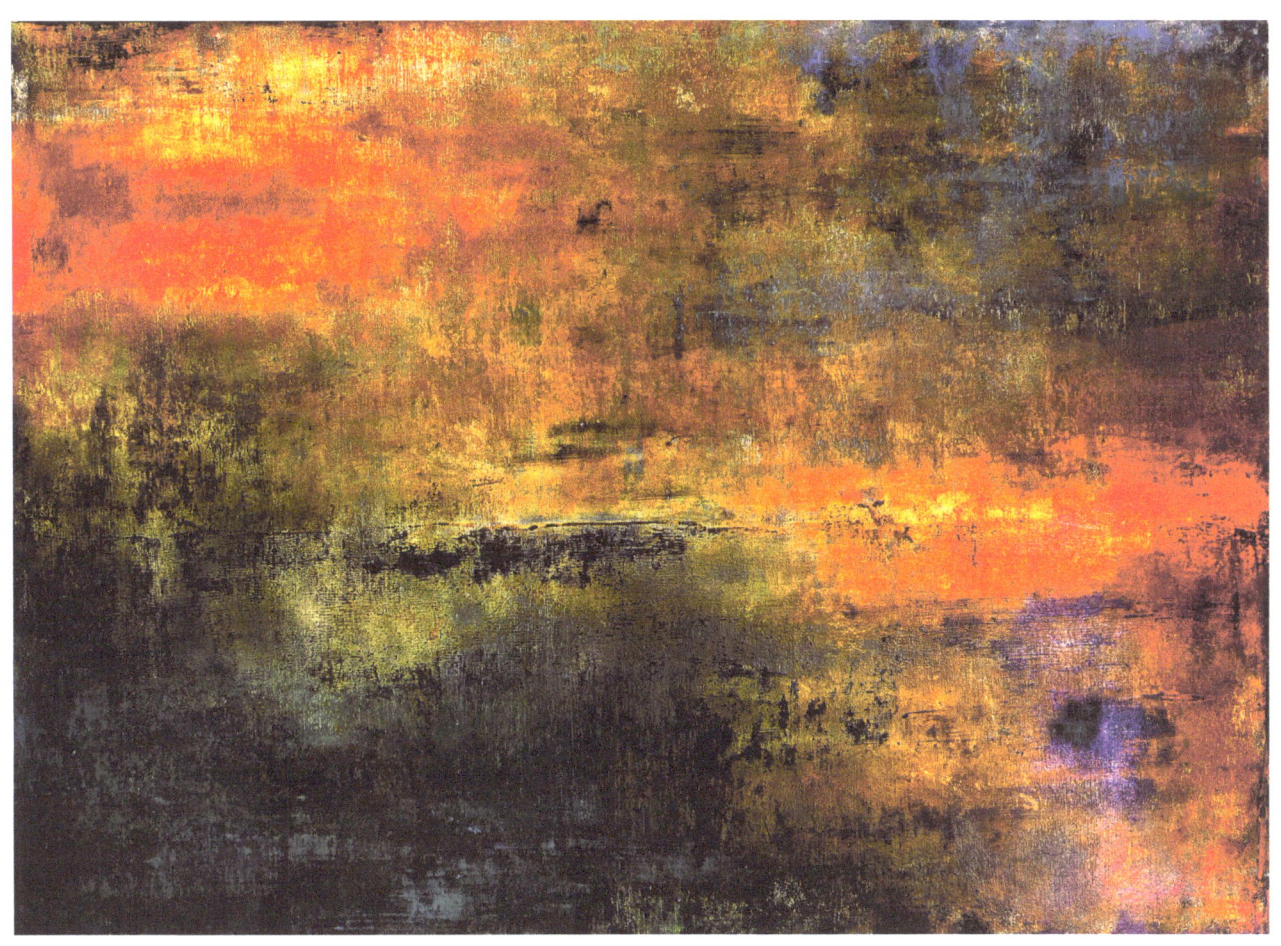

Oil on wood
120 x 80 cm
In private collection

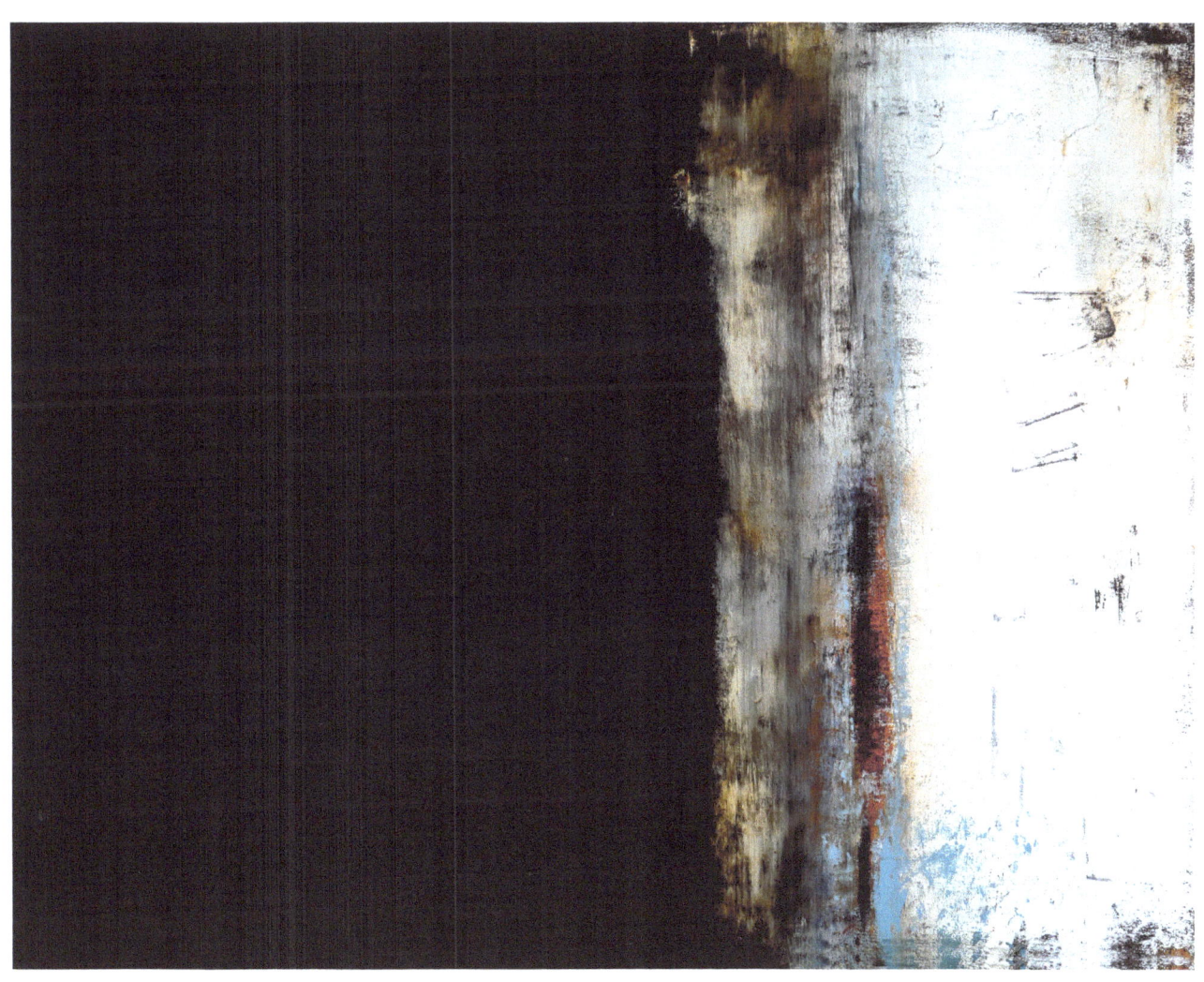

Oil on canvas
120 x 80 cm
In private collection

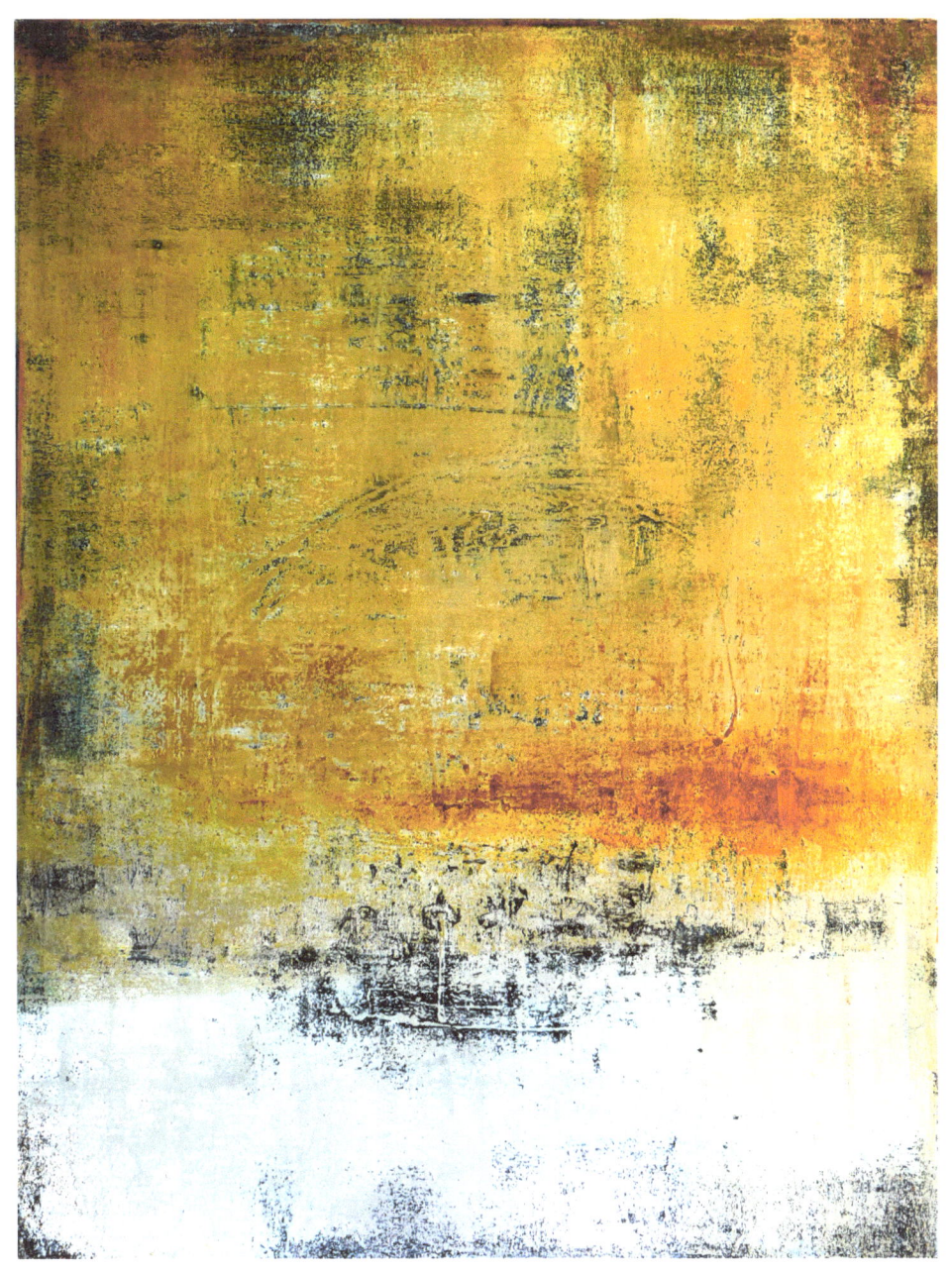

Oil on canvas
120 x 80 cm
In private collection

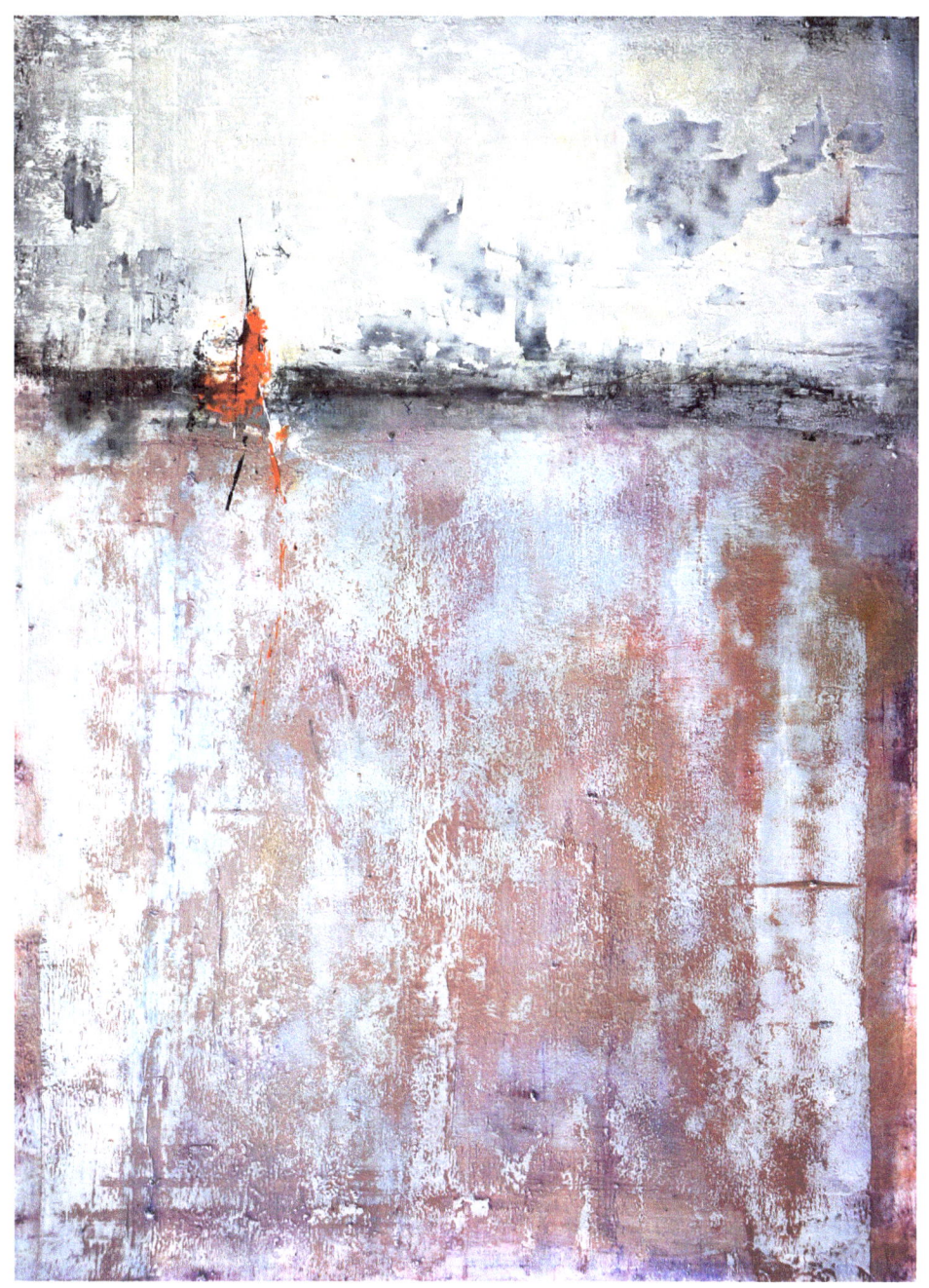

Oil on paper
77 x 55 cm
In private collection

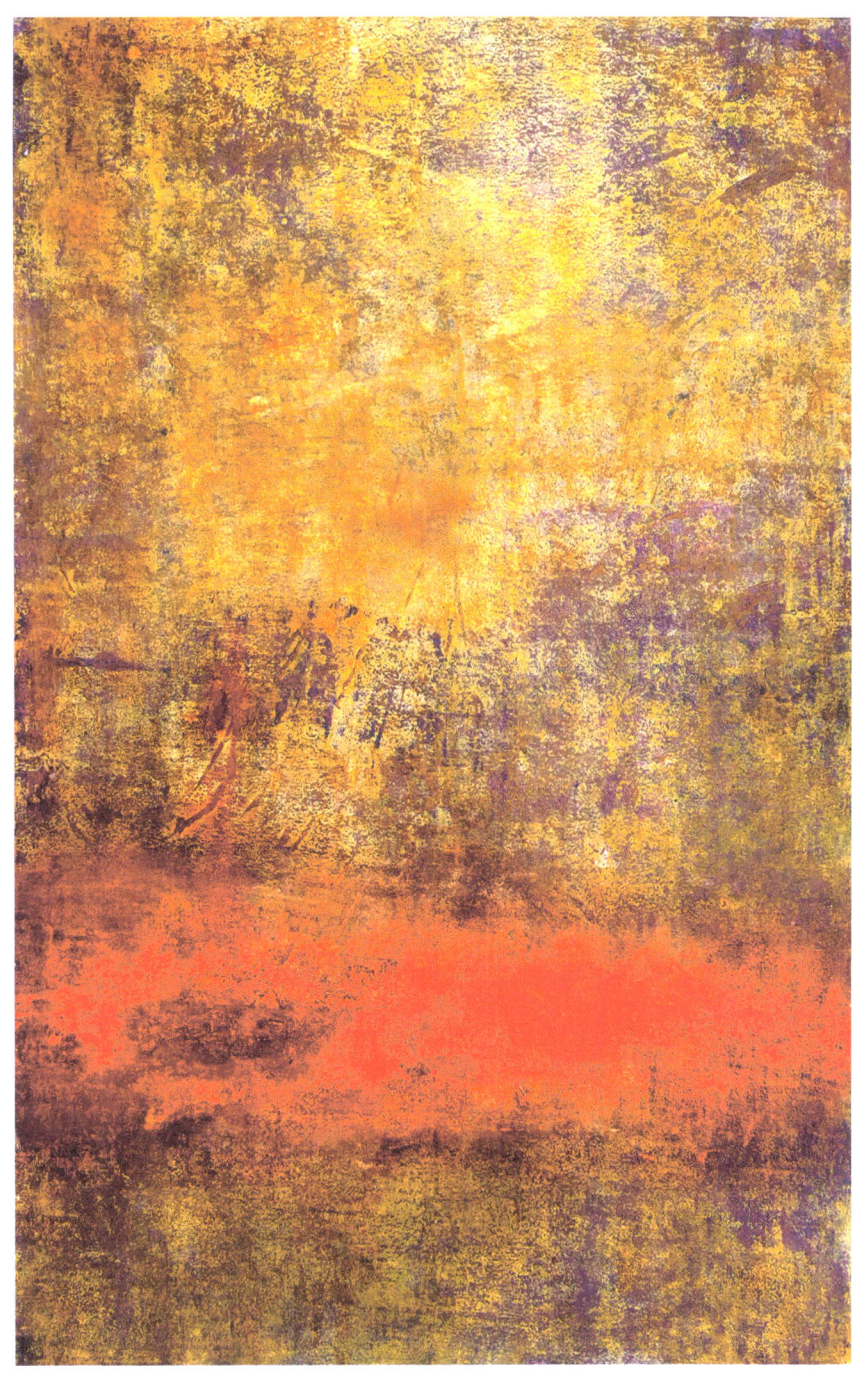

Oil on wood
120 x 80 cm
In private collection

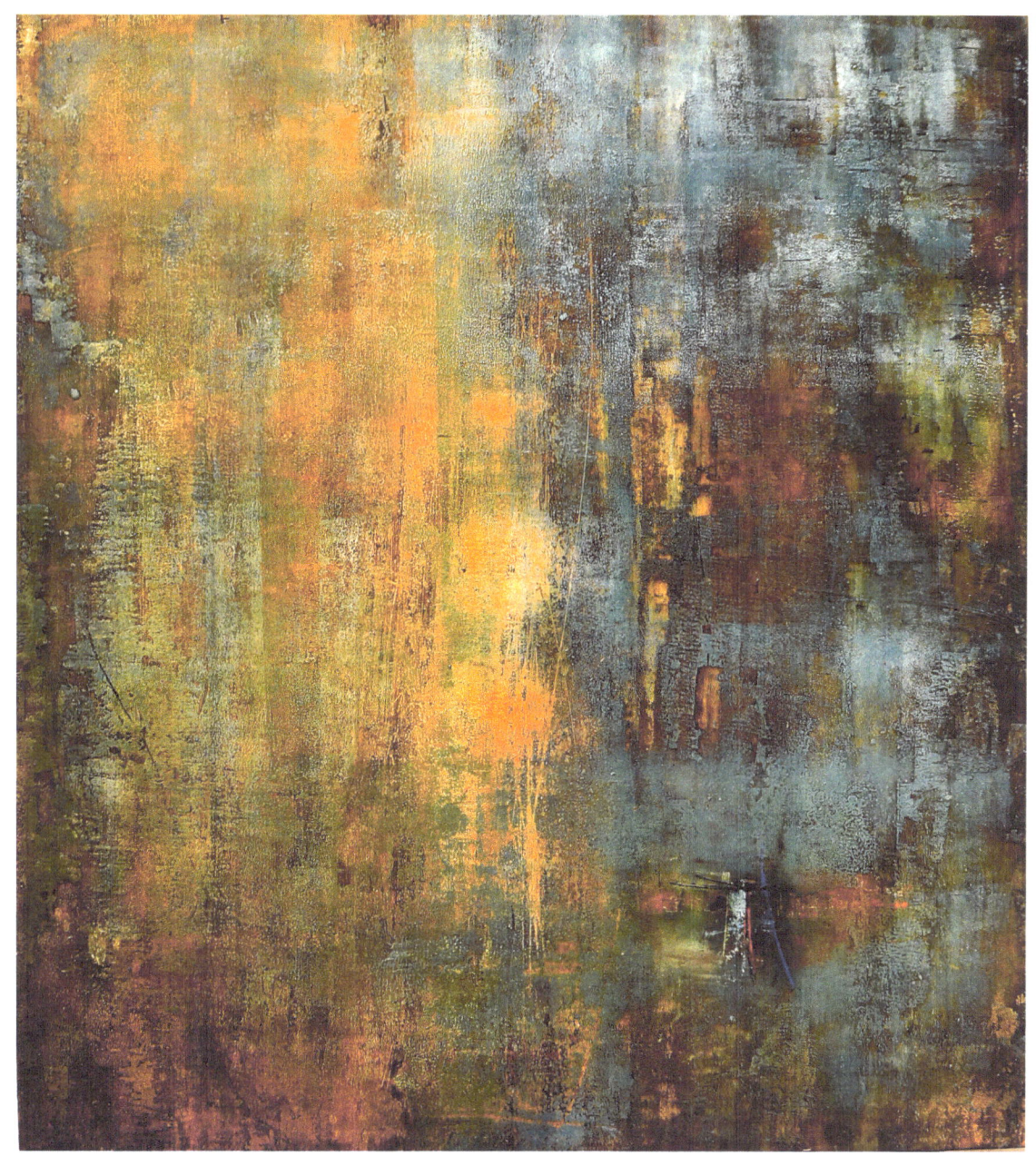

Oil on wood
120 x 120 cm
In private collection

Oil on paper
195 x 100 cm
In private collection

Oil on canvas
80 x 63 cm
In private collection

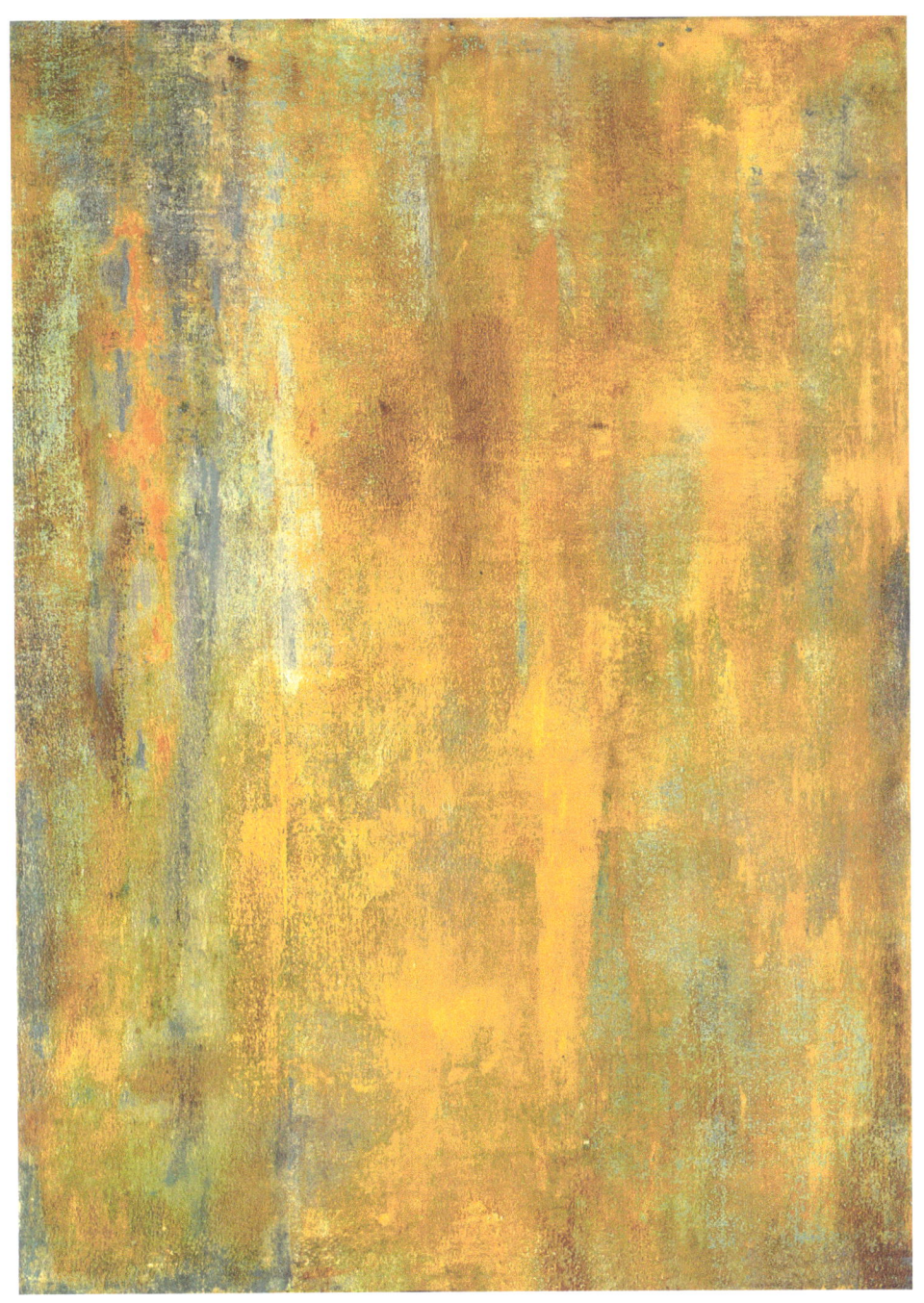

Oil on canvas
120 x 80 cm
In private collection

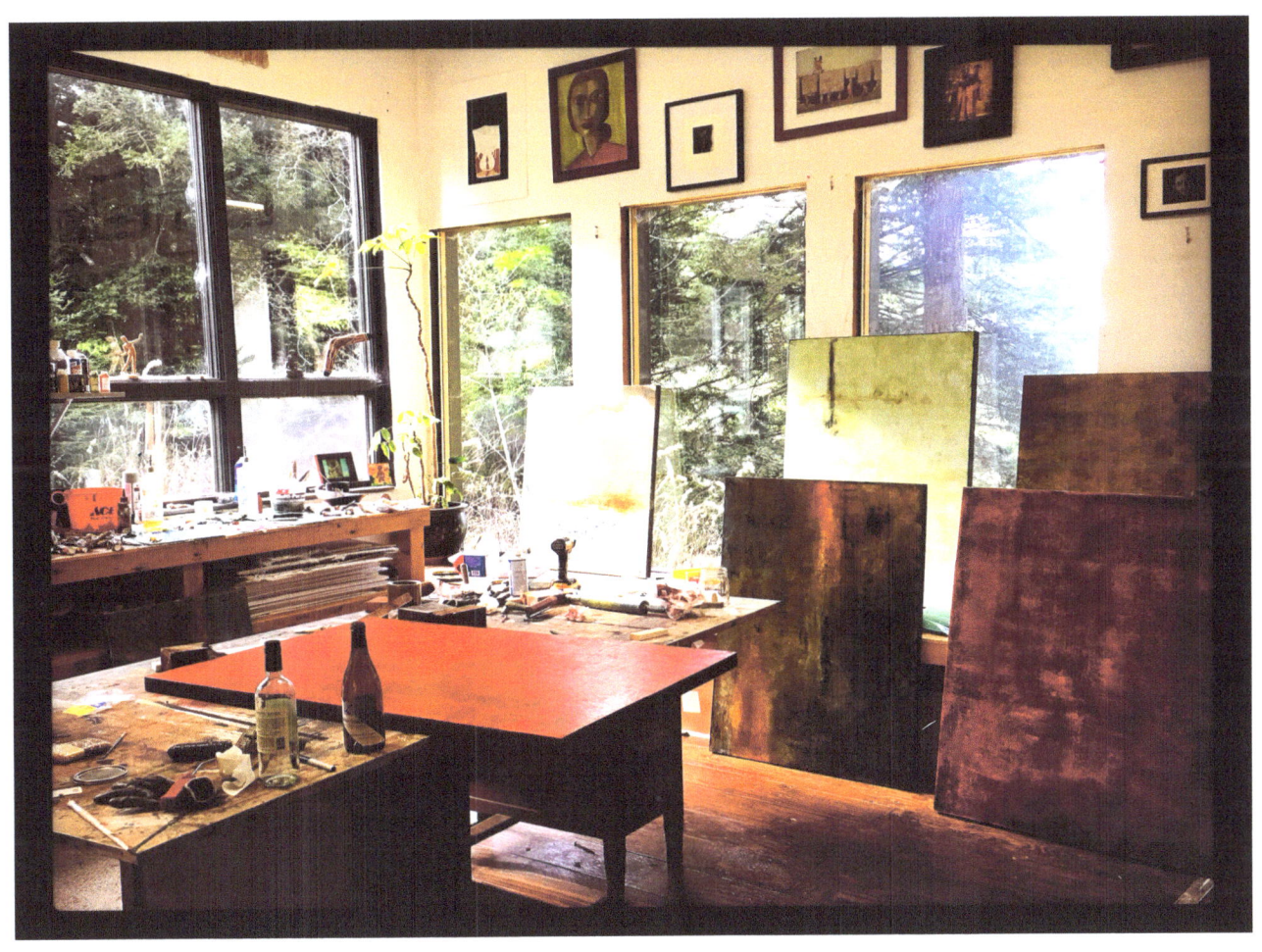

A corner of my studio in Freshwater, nestled in the California redwoods.

www.ingramcontent.com/pod-product-compliance
Lightning Source LLC
Chambersburg PA
CBHW051046180526
45172CB00002B/536